Color and Wavelengths

Published in the United States of America by Cherry Lake Publishing
Ann Arbor, Michigan
www.cherrylakepublishing.com

Reading Adviser: Marla Conn MS, Ed., Literacy specialist, Read-Ability, Inc.
Content Adviser: Brittany Burchard M.Ed., Science teacher
Book Design: Jennifer Wahi
Illustrator: Jeff Bane

Library of Congress Cataloging-in-Publication Data

Names: Bell, Samantha, author. | Bane, Jeff, 1957- illustrator.
Title: Color and wavelengths / by Samantha Bell ; illustrator: Jeff Bane.
Description: Ann Arbor, Michigan : Cherry Lake Publishing, [2018] | Series:
  My world of science | Includes index. | Audience: K to grade 3.
Identifiers: LCCN 2017031589| ISBN 9781534107274 (hardcover) | ISBN
  1534107274 (hardcover) | ISBN 9781534108264 (pbk.) | ISBN 1534108262
  (pbk.) | ISBN 9781534109254 (pdf) | ISBN 1534109250 (pdf) | ISBN
  9781534120242 (hosted ebook) | ISBN 1534120246 (hosted ebook)
Subjects: LCSH: Color--Juvenile literature. | Light--Wave-length--Juvenile
  literature.
Classification: LCC QC495.5 .B45 2018 | DDC 535.6--dc23
LC record available at https://lccn.loc.gov/2017031589

Printed in the United States of America
Corporate Graphics

table of contents

About the author: Samantha Bell has written and illustrated over 60 books for children. She lives in South Carolina with her family and pets.

About the illustrator: Jeff Bane and his two business partners own a studio along the American River in Folsom, California, home of the 1849 Gold Rush. When Jeff's not sketching or illustrating for clients, he's either swimming or kayaking in the river to relax.

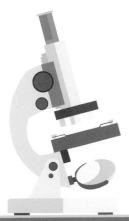

Light is moving when it shines.

It moves like a wave on the water. We see light waves as colors.

Each color has a different **wavelength**.

Some waves are short. These are **violet**, **indigo**, blue, and green.

Some waves are long. These are yellow, orange, and red.

What is your favorite color?

All of the colors together make white light.

White light from the sun travels
through the air.

The light from the sun is white.
The light from a **flashlight** is
white, too.

Sometimes sunlight breaks apart. We see the colors when this happens. It makes a **rainbow** in the sky.

When have you seen a rainbow?

Some **scientists** study color and wavelengths. They ask questions. They look for answers.

What would you like to study next?

glossary & index

glossary

flashlight (FLASH-lite) a small light powered by batteries

indigo (IN-dih-go) a dark violet-blue color

rainbow (RAYN-boh) a curved pattern of colors in the sky

scientists (SYE-uhn-tists) people who study nature and the world we live in

violet (VYE-uh-lit) a blue-purple color

wavelength (WAYV-lengkth) the distance from the top of one light wave to the top of the next one

index